Pipsqueaks, Slowpokes, and Stinkers

Celebrating Animal Underdogs

Melissa Stewart

Illustrated by Stephanie Laberis

PEACHTREE

ATLANTA

Everyone loves elephants. They're so big and strong.

Everyone respects cheetahs. They're so fast and fierce.

But this book isn't about animals we admire. It's about the unsung underdogs of the animal world. Don't you think it's time someone paid attention to them?

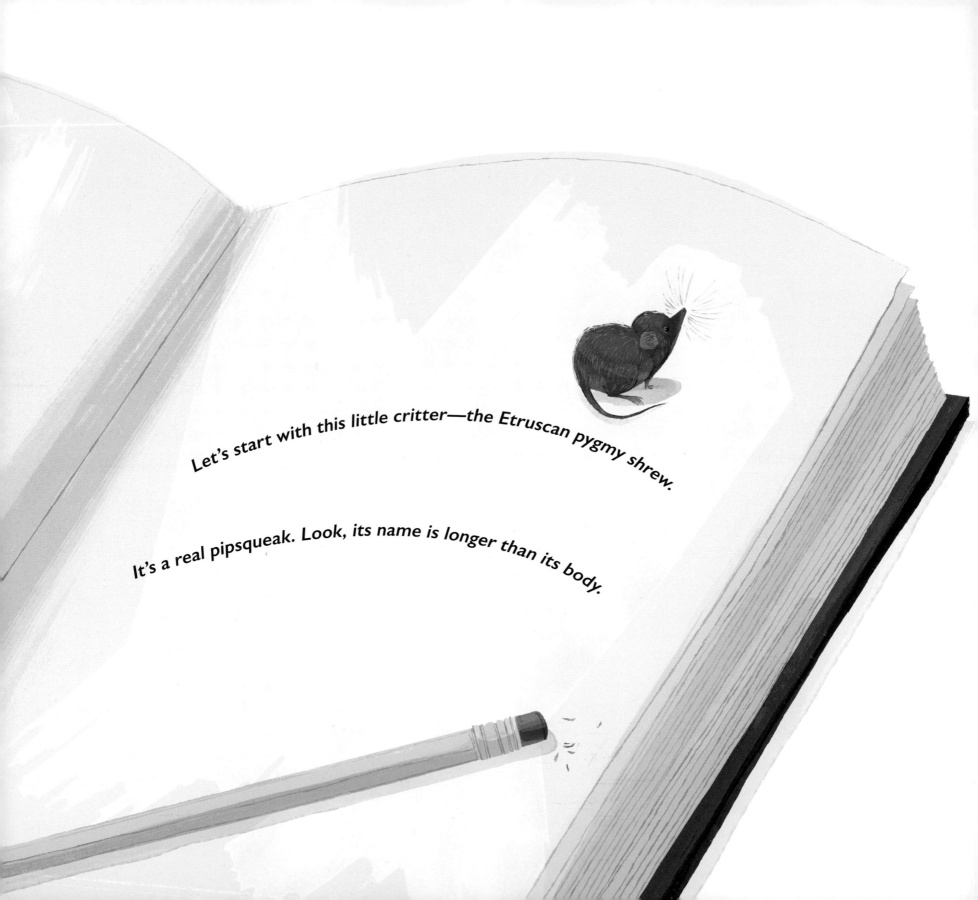

Let's start with this little critter—the Etruscan pygmy shrew.

It's a real pipsqueak. Look, its name is longer than its body.

An Amau frog is even smaller.
It could perch on your pinkie
with room to spare.

How can these puny peewees survive
in a world full of predators with huge
teeth and razor-sharp claws?

Believe it or not,

size is on their side.

When hulking hunters

get too close,

our little heroes

slip into small,

secret spots

their enemies

can't reach.

It takes a Galápagos tortoise almost six hours to travel a mile. What a slowpoke!

Most people can walk that far in just twenty minutes.

Why don't these creeping critters get a move on?
Because tortoises don't need speed. Their hard,
strong shells protect them from predators.

Pee-eeew! What's that stinking stench? Meet the hoatzin.

This strange bird eats lots of leaves, and as it digests them,

its body reeks worse than cow manure.

Feeling sick to your stomach?

Then you might not want to know about zorillas.

Their nasty spray is stronger than a skunk's,

and the awful odor lasts longer.

Should hoatzins and zorillas clean up their act?

No way! These stinkers are sending their enemies a powerful message. When hungry hunters sniff a whiff of a hoatzin's body odor, they lose their appetites. And when predators smell a zorilla's stinky spray, they skedaddle.

Ever seen an okapi? If not, you aren't alone.

It's one of the shyest animals on Earth.

Why does the horse-sized creature
choose to live alone in shadowy forests?
So it can stay safe. When an okapi senses
danger, it silently sneaks out of sight.

Koalas and giant armadillos
snooze for eighteen hours a day.
Boy, are they lazy!

Little brown bats get
even more shut-eye.
They rest for twenty hours a day.
Should these sleepy slackers
change their ways?

Nope. Napping is the secret to their survival success.
Because koalas, giant armadillos, and little brown bats spend so
much time resting, they don't need to get as much energy from
their food as more active animals.

What's the world's clumsiest critter? Probably
the western fence lizard. As it skitters along tree
branches, it sometimes loses its balance and falls
to the forest floor. *Thud*.

Why does the little lizard run so fast that it stumbles over its feet? Because it needs speed to catch quick-crawling spiders and insects. Wouldn't you rather take a tumble once in a while than starve to death?

In winter, a walrus's thick layer of fat can weigh more than 400 pounds.

Seals and sea lions fatten up too. What a bunch of blubbery blobs!

Think these plump lumps should go on a diet?

Think again! Blubber helps walruses, seals, and sea lions stay warm in chilly ocean water.

It also provides energy during periods when the animals can't hunt for food.

Now feast your eyes on these curious critters . . . or maybe you'd rather not. After all, naked mole rats are a real eyesore.

They use their giant buckteeth to dig for tasty roots. And their furless bodies help them beat the heat in their hot desert home.

Should naked mole rats rush out to see
an orthodontist and buy a cozy coat?
You decide.

It's easy to admire animals that are big and fast, lean and graceful.

You might even be tempted to make fun of creatures that seem slow or lazy or shy.

But consider this: What seems like a weakness could actually be a strength.

Every animal on Earth—from tiny shrews and stinky zorillas to shy okapis and

clumsy lizards—has its own special way of surviving.

More About the Underdogs

The **Etruscan pygmy shrew** hunts at night, using its long whiskers to sense earthworms, insects, and other tasty treats. When hungry owls swoop overhead, it darts into rocky crevices or huddles under shrubs.

Digesting leaves is no easy task, so a **hoatzin** has a larger digestive system than other birds. As bacteria in a hoatzin's gut break down the plant material, they give off gases that make the bird stink.

What happens if an **Amau frog** doesn't have time to hop to safety? It sits still and hopes for the best. Its small size and earthy skin patterns make it hard for most predators to spot.

A **zorilla** has a lot in common with a skunk, but it's more closely related to a weasel. Its stinky spray makes a predator's nose and mouth burn. It can also make enemies temporarily blind.

The **Galápagos tortoise** can live up to 150 years. That means the super-slow reptile has plenty of time to get where it wants to go.

The **okapi** is closely related to the not-so-shy giraffe. Its dark body helps it hide in its shadowy rain-forest home. The stripes on an okapi's legs break up its outline, making it even harder to spot.

A **koala** spends its waking hours greedily gorging on eucalyptus leaves. But its food isn't very nutritious. Even though the fuzzy furball has a sleepy lifestyle, it still has to eat a lot just to stay alive.

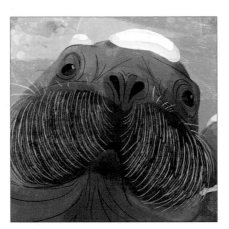

Thanks to its thick blubber, a **walrus** can survive at temperatures as low as −31 degrees Fahrenheit (−35 degrees Celsius).

Giant armadillos and **little brown bats** are insect eaters that hunt at night. Because they rest so much, they don't have to eat as much food as other animals their size.

During mating season, **seals** and **sea lions** form huge colonies on rocky beaches. The adults may go for weeks without food. Luckily, they get all the energy they need from their thick, fatty blubber.

The speedy critters that **western fence lizards** hunt can't survive chilly winter weather. How do the blue-bellied reptiles survive? By spending the coolest months of the year hibernating underground.

The **naked mole rat** may look strange, but its body is perfectly designed for life underground. Besides tunneling teeth, it has tiny eyes and needs very little oxygen to survive.

Selected Sources

Amazing Animals of the World. New York, NY: Scholastic, 2006.

Animal Diversity Web (*http://animaldiversity.org*)

Breed, Michael D. and Janice Moore, eds. *Encyclopedia of Animal Behavior.* Waltham, MA: Academic Press, 2010.

*Carwardine, Mark. *Natural History Museum Book of Animal Records.* Richmond Hill, ON, Canada: Firefly Books, 2013.

"Meet the World's Smallest Vertebrate," *Science.* Washington, DC: American Association for the Advancement of Science, January 20, 2012, p. 269.

*Jenkins, Steve. *The Animal Book: A Collection of the Fastest, Fiercest, Toughest, Cleverest, Shyest—and Most Surprising—Animals on Earth.* Boston: Houghton Mifflin Harcourt, 2013.

*National Geographic: Animals (*http://www.nationalgeographic.com/animals/*)

Stewart, Melissa. Personal observations recorded in journals, 1989–present.

*Recommended for young readers.

For any child who is being bullied right now—
what others see as a weakness may actually be your strength.
Don't give up.

—M. S.

To the pipsqueaks, slowpokes, and stinkers that have come
through the doors of Lindsay Wildlife Hospital. Every single one of you.

—S. L.

Published by
PEACHTREE PUBLISHERS
1700 Chattahoochee Avenue
Atlanta, Georgia 30318-2112
www.peachtree-online.com

Text © 2018 by Melissa Stewart
Illustrations © 2018 by Stephanie Laberis

Design and composition by Nicola Simmonds Carmack

The illustrations were created in Adobe Photoshop CC.

Edited by Vicky Holifield

Printed in February 2018 by Tien Wah Press in Malaysia
10 9 8 7 6 5 4 3 2 1
First Edition
ISBN 978-1-56145-936-0

Library of Congress Cataloging-in-Publication Data

Names: Stewart, Melissa, author. | Laberis, Steph, illustrator.
Title: Pipsqueaks, slowpokes, and stinkers : celebrating animal underdogs / written by Melissa Stewart ; illustrated by Stephanie Laberis.
Description: First edition. | Atlanta : Peachtree Publishers, [2018] | Audience: Age 4-8. | Audience: Grade K to 3. | Includes bibliographical references.
Identifiers: LCCN 2017017992 | ISBN 9781561459360
Subjects: LCSH: Animal behavior—Juvenile literature. | Animals—Miscellanea—Juvenile literature.
Classification: LCC QL751.5 .S745 2018 | DDC 591—dc23 LC record available at *https://lccn.loc.gov/2017017992*

For information about the process of writing this book and related teaching materials, please visit *www.melissa-stewart.com.*